Dyslexia

Dr. Alvin Silverstein,

Virginia Silverstein, and

Laura Silverstein Nunn

My Health

Franklin Watts

A Division of Scholastic Inc.

New York • Toronto • London • Auckland • Sydney

Mexico City • New Delhi • Hong Kong

Danbury, Connecticut

Photographs©: Liaison Agency, Inc.: 4 (Dean Berry), 35 (J-L Bulcao), 23 (Brooks Kraft), 10 (Roger Viollet/Gamma Presse); Photo Researchers, NY: 38 (Ken Cavanagh), 16 (Robert Finken), 6 (Richard Hutchings), 8, 13 (Will & Deni McIntyre/SS), 21 (Wellcome Dept. of Cognitive Neurology/SPL), 18, 20 (Medivisuals/SS), 24 (Saturn Stills/SPL), 30 (Hattie Young/SPL); PhotoEdit: 11, 36, 37 (Mary Kate Denny), 26, 28 (Will Hart), 7, 32 (Stephen McBrady), 27 (Michael Newman), 39 (Steve Skjold); The Image Works: 14 (Ellen Senisi); Woodfin Camp & Associates: 12, 17 (Susan Lapides).

Cartoons by Rick Stromoski

Library of Congress Cataloging-in-Publication Data

Silverstein, Alvin.
    Dyslexia / by Alvin Silverstein, Virginia Silverstein, and Laura Silverstein Nunn.
        p.   cm.—(My Health)
    Includes bibliographical references and index.
    ISBN 0-531-11862-2 (lib. bdg.)   0-531-16560-4 (pbk.)
    1. Dyslexia—Juvenile literature. [1. Dyslexia.]
I. Silverstein, Virginia B. II. Nunn, Laura Silverstein III. Title IV. Series.
RC394.W6 S54 2001
616.85'53—dc21

                                      00-051359
                                      CIP
                                      AC

Contents

Reading Problems

Do you have trouble reading? Maybe you get distracted and lose your place. Or maybe you have trouble remembering what you've just read. Does your handwriting ever get so sloppy that your teacher can't make out what you wrote? Have you ever misspelled words because you were careless or because you just forgot the correct spelling?

Everybody makes mistakes like these from time to time. It's perfectly normal. Most people catch their errors right away and correct them. But some people have reading and writing problems like these *all the time*. It's not because they are lazy or stupid. It's because they have a learning disorder called **dyslexia**.

Did You Know...

A learning disability is a condition that makes it difficult to learn. Dyslexia is the most common learning disability. About 2.4 million children in the United States have learning disabilities, and 80 to 85 percent of them have dyslexia.

◀ **Learning to read is important, but it can be hard at first.**

Dyslexia is a condition that makes it hard for people to read, write, spell, speak, and listen. Dyslexics—people who have dyslexia—cannot figure out language the way most people do. Their brain has trouble making the connection between the way letters look on a page and the sounds of words. As a result, people with this condition may not be able to understand what words and sentences mean when they try to read.

Kids with dyslexia may have a very hard time in school. They may think they are stupid, even though they actually may be very smart. After trying and failing many times, some just give up trying to learn. Some

Even if school seems difficult and frustrating sometimes, don't give up.

Individual attention can help a child who has trouble learning to read.

may develop behavior problems, disrupting the class and making it difficult for other children to learn.

That's why it is important to identify children who are having reading or learning problems as early as possible. If you or someone you know has dyslexia, there are things that can be done to help. Experts have worked out ways to make learning easier for dyslexics. There are tricks dyslexics can use that will train their brains to make sense out of the words they read.

Read on to find out more about dyslexia. You'll find out what causes dyslexia and learn how reading problems can be overcome.

Who Has Dyslexia?

Dyslexia affects 5 to 15 percent of the people living in the United States. That adds up to millions of people. In fact, there is probably someone in your class at school who has dyslexia. Experts say that it affects 1 out of 5 schoolchildren.

There's probably a child in your class who is just as frustrated as this dyslexic child.

Anyone can have dyslexia. It affects people of all races and all nationalities. Dyslexia is detected more often in boys, but the condition actually affects about the same number of girls. Boys with learning problems tend to misbehave in class so they are identified by teachers more often. Girls with learning problems, on the other hand, tend to keep to themselves and do not attract attention.

Dyslexia is often **inherited**. People who have dyslexia are born with it. You are more likely to have dyslexia if one of your parents, grandparents, aunts, uncles, or some other family member has it. Scientists have found that certain **genes** may make some people more likely to develop the condition. Genes are very small structures that carry traits passed on from parents to children.

Dyslexics may feel stupid when they have problems learning in school, but there is actually no link between dyslexia and intelligence. Many dyslexics are very smart and creative. You might be surprised to know that people with dyslexia have become successful doctors, teachers, writers, lawyers, movie stars, or athletes.

Did You Know...

Kids who have dyslexia do not "grow out of it." It is a condition they will have to deal with for the rest of their lives.

Some of the most important and famous people in history had dyslexia. For example, the scientist Albert Einstein, one of the world's greatest geniuses, had dyslexia. So did Thomas Edison, who invented the electric light, and Alexander Graham Bell, the inventor of the telephone. United States President Woodrow Wilson had dyslexia too—and before he became president, he was a college professor.

Albert Einstein, one of the smartest people of all time, had dyslexia.

Some Famous Dyslexics

Agatha Christie (mystery novelist)

Benjamin Franklin (scientist/inventor)

Cher (singer, actress)

Danny Glover (actor)

Dustin Hoffman (actor)

George Patton (army general)

Greg Louganis (Olympic diver)

Hans Christian Andersen (writer)

Henry Winkler (actor/producer/director)

Jack Nicholson (actor)

Jay Leno (late-night talk-show host)

Jewel (singer)

Leonardo da Vinci (artist)

Robin Williams (actor/comedian)

Sylvester Stallone (actor)

Tom Cruise (actor)

Walt Disney (cartoonist)

Whoopi Goldberg (actress/comedian)

What Is Dyslexia?

The word *dyslexia* comes from two Greek words—*dys*, meaning "difficulty," and *lex* meaning "word." People with dyslexia have difficulty in using words or language. Basically, dyslexics have trouble making the connection between symbols—letters of the alphabet—and the sounds we make when we say them.

This teacher is helping a dyslexic boy make the connection between letters and sounds.

This teacher and her student are practicing making a vowel sound.

Think of a printed page as a message written in code. In this code, each letter stands for a sound used when people speak. Most children learn to read by cracking the "language code." They figure out what letters look and sound like when they are put together to create words.

The sounds we use to make words are called **phonemes** (FOH-neemz). The two main kinds of phonemes are vowels and consonants. Vowels are sounds you make with your mouth open. You use your lips, tongue, and teeth to form the sounds of consonants.

In dyslexia, certain areas of the brain have trouble figuring out this language code. For instance, a dyslexic may not recognize a simple word, such as "cat." The word "cat" is made up of three phonemes—"kuh," "aah," and "tuh." This seems clear to most people, but dyslexics hear "cat" as one sound. As a result, they don't use the parts of the word—the phonemes—to sound it out when they see the letters.

Also, for many dyslexics, the letters that make up a word get mixed up. For instance, the word "bat" may be confused with "tab," or the word "brain" may appear as "brian." So dyslexics often have trouble understanding what printed words mean. They may also have trouble writing. They may spell words incorrectly or have trouble expressing their ideas in a way that other people can understand. Other problems may develop as well.

Some dyslexic students have problems with writing.

The following list includes some possible signs of dyslexia.

- Difficulty connecting letters with sounds
- Difficulty dividing words into *syllables*
- Confusion or reversal of letters and numbers, such as "sing" and "sign"; "left" and "felt"; or "67" and "76"

It takes a lot of practice to overcome the reversal of letters and numbers.

- Confusion between letters that look similar, such as b and d; and p and q
- Difficulty remembering what has been read
- Difficulty spelling
- Difficulty with handwriting
- Difficulty copying words or numbers from the chalkboard or a book
- Difficulty reading aloud
- Difficulty expressing thoughts and ideas verbally or in written form
- Confusion about directions relating to space or time, such as right and left, up and down, early and late, yesterday and tomorrow, months and days
- Difficulty following instructions
- Difficulty rhyming

A person with dyslexia may have just a few of these problems, or many of them. Every dyslexic has his or her own individual combination of difficulties. The signs or symptoms of dyslexia are mild in some people and severe in others.

Activity 1:
What's It Like to Have Dyslexia?

Can you imagine looking at a bunch of words on a page and not being able to make any sense out of them? You can get an idea of what a dyslexic might see by holding a book up to a mirror. You'll see that the letters are reversed. Try to read the words you see in the mirror. It's not easy. Now turn the book upside down and hold it up to the mirror. That's another way words may appear to dyslexics. How do they look to you? Confusing? That's exactly what reading is to dyslexics—confusing.

This kind of frustration can make a child feel like giving up.

Dyslexics often feel stupid because they can't read or figure things out as easily as other kids can. Their teachers may also consider these kids slow or mentally handicapped. This can hurt a child's **self-esteem**. Dyslexics may feel that they can't handle school or the embarrassment. In fact, studies have shown that dyslexia is the main reason for school dropouts in the United States. That's a shame because many dyslexics are actually very smart. Remember all those famous people in the list on page 10!

It's All in the Brain

Scientists used to think that dyslexia was caused by eye problems because dyslexics mix up letters and confuse similar words. In fact, the condition used to be called "word blindness." But dyslexia has nothing to do with poor vision. A dyslexic's eyes work normally. Today, many experts believe that dyslexia develops because something in the brain isn't working in the same way as it does in people who read easily. The problem is that the brain has trouble relating the images of printed letters to the sounds of spoken words.

This woman is helping two dyslexic children learn how to read.

Each part of your brain does a special job. The outermost layer of your brain is called the **cerebral cortex**. You use that part to think, remember, and make decisions. You also use it to understand and form words and to control body movements. The cerebral cortex receives messages from your ears, eyes, nose, taste buds, and skin. It lets you know what is going on in the world around you.

This is what your brain would look like if it were sliced in half. The cerebral cortex is the largest part of a person's brain.

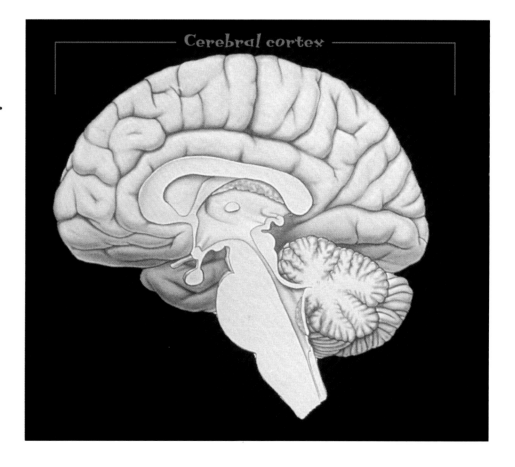

Cerebral cortex

Your brain is made up of two hemispheres, or halves—the right and the left. Each side specializes in certain activities. In general, the left hemisphere, or left brain, is the verbal half. It allows you to read and write, speak easily, and do difficult math problems. You use your right brain to read common words, do simple math problems, and understand simple verbal instructions. The right brain is also involved in artistic activities. It helps you understand and appreciate shapes, texture, and color as well as musical rhythms and melodies. The two halves of the brain work together to make you a well-rounded person.

Left Brain Versus Right Brain

People usually use one side of the brain more than the other. Most people are left-brain thinkers. That is, they are usually better at reading, writing, and other verbal skills than at expressing themselves artistically. Many dyslexics, however, are right-brain thinkers. They may have trouble reading and writing, but they are often very artistic and creative. That's why many dyslexics have become important people in society—artists, poets, inventors, actors, and even presidents.

ART
MUSIC
POETRY
KEEP RIGHT

These are the parts of the brain involved in reading and speaking words.

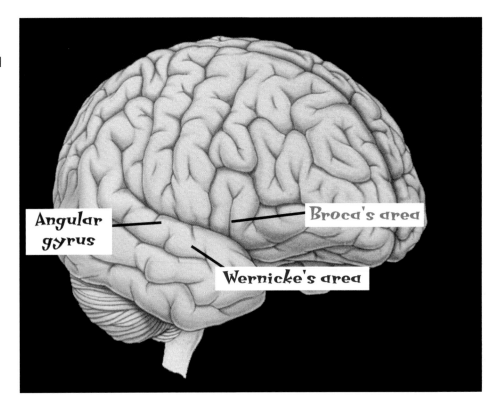

Angular gyrus

Broca's area

Wernicke's area

The left brain contains two important areas that help turn sounds into meaningful speech—**Wernicke's area** (in the back of the brain) and **Broca's area** (in the front of the brain). Together, these areas help you figure out the meaning of sounds and form spoken words. Wernicke's area is involved in understanding the meanings of words. It also helps you string words together to form sentences. Then your Broca's area directs the muscle movement so that you can speak the words.

When you read a word, the vision center in your brain turns signals sent from the eyes into an image, or picture, of that word. An area in the brain just behind Wernicke's area, called the **angular gyrus**, turns the image of the word into sounds. Wernicke's area then figures out the meaning of the sounds. Now you can link the letters you see on a page to sounds and combine the sounds to form words.

Scientists have been able to learn about dyslexia by using special pictures of the brain called **MRI** and **PET scans**. These scans allow scientists to watch brain activity and find out what areas of the brain are not working properly. Researchers have learned that the left hemisphere—the area devoted to reading—works differently in the brains of dyslexics.

Normally, when a person reads words, there is a lot of brain activity in the

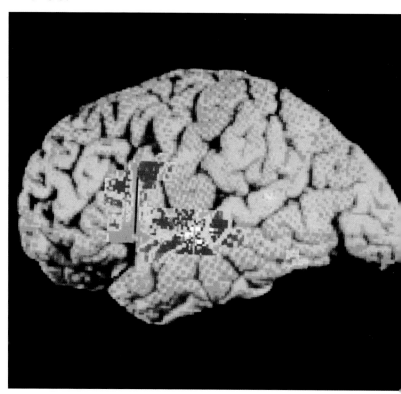

In a PET scan, active parts of the brain light up. This scan was taken while a person listened to sounds and tried to recognize words.

language areas, including Wernicke's area, Broca's area, and the angular gyrus. However, MRI and PET scans of people with dyslexia show very little brain activity in Wernicke's area—the part of the brain devoted to forming and understanding the meanings of words. The angular gyrus also has a low level of brain activity. But there is greater activity in Broca's area—the part of the brain involved in speaking words.

Scientists are working hard to find out more about dyslexia. They hope they can learn to identify children who are at risk for developing reading problems. This would make it possible to catch the condition early and begin treatment before the child has to deal with frustrations at school.

Diagnosing Dyslexia

It's not easy to decide whether a child has dyslexia. Dyslexia is not like a broken arm, for example, where an X ray can show the problem. Dyslexia is not caused by a germ that can be picked up by a blood test. That's why dyslexia is sometimes called a "hidden disability." People with this learning disorder are often told, "You're not trying hard enough." Actually, many of them are working harder than most people but, for them, learning how to read is like running into a brick wall.

Is this girl dyslexic? Sometimes it's hard to tell.

Many children with dyslexia learn how to hide their reading problem. Sometimes they pretend to understand what people are saying, or they may direct their energy to other activities, such as art classes or school plays. Some kids get so frustrated that they misbehave, which makes teachers think they have a behavior problem rather than a learning problem.

The process of diagnosing dyslexia usually starts with a physical exam. Some conditions may be confused with dyslexia. For example, hearing problems can make it

Does this child have a hearing problem or a reading problem? A doctor can help to find out.

seem like a child doesn't understand what people are saying. The child's eyes should be checked too. Poor vision can make reading difficult.

When health problems have been ruled out, the doctor may send the child to a psychologist or a learning specialist. The specialist will ask the child and his or her parents questions about their family history and about the child's behavior at home and at school. The specialist may ask: "Are you upset about going to school?" "Do you have trouble with spelling or reading aloud?" "Did other family members have problems reading and spelling when they were in school?" "Do you confuse left and right?" "Do you have trouble following instructions when you're playing a game?"

Did You Know...

Behavior problems could also be a sign of **attention deficit disorder (ADD)**. People with ADD have difficulty concentrating, paying attention, or controlling their behavior. Some children have both dyslexia and ADD. These kids have a lot of trouble learning.

After gathering information about the child, the specialist will give the child a number of tests. These usually include an intelligence test that measures thinking abilities and a language test that checks the child's ability to understand spoken and written language. A reading test will help the specialist figure out the child's reading level and understanding of what he or she has read. Other useful tests may include a spelling test, a math test, a

Tests of reading and writing can help to identify what kind of learning problems a child has.

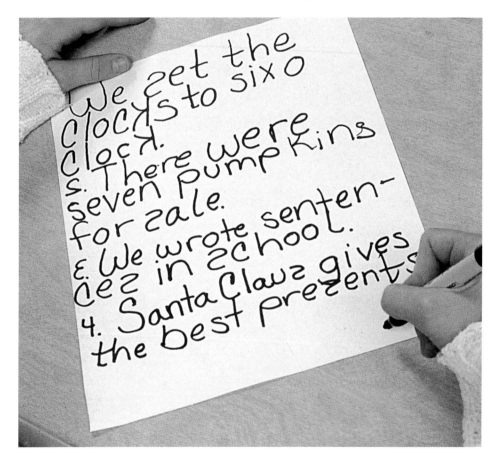

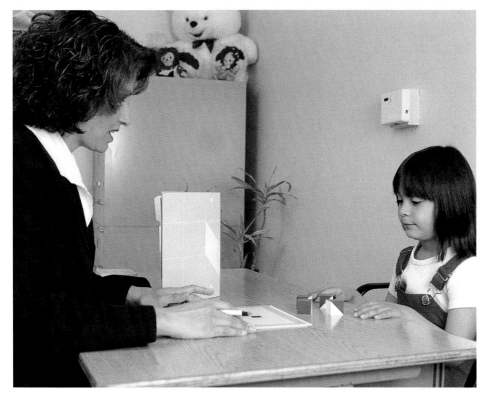

A learning specialist may also test a child's ability to think logically and organize.

sequencing test (checking the ability to put things in the right order), and a test to find out the child's understanding of directions, such as left and right, up and down. A self-esteem test that shows how the child feels about himself or herself may also be helpful.

The psychologist or learning specialist should also talk to the child's teacher about school performance before making a diagnosis. Getting a diagnosis of dyslexia is often a huge relief. Now the child can get help and learn how to overcome the condition.

Getting Help

There is no cure for dyslexia. But dyslexics can learn ways to improve their language skills and do better in school.

Dyslexics need to seek help from a teacher or therapist who is specially trained to teach children with learning problems. Since their condition varies, dyslexics do best with individual attention. They also

This boy is excited about overcoming his reading problem. He has worked hard and received lots of one-on-one help from his teachers.

need to be taught in a structured, well-organized environment. The more lessons they have each week, the more they will improve. With a lot of patience and motivation, dyslexics can retrain their way of thinking.

The Younger the Better

It is usually easier to help young kids overcome dyslexia. For example, a child who is diagnosed with dyslexia in elementary school is more likely to succeed—and can overcome the problem more quickly—than a dyslexic who is not diagnosed until high school. One reason could be that older students have faced more frustrations and failures. Their self-esteem is low, and they may have lost their motivation. Without motivation, learning becomes difficult. Another reason may be that younger students are more open to learning and absorb information more easily than older students.

Many different kinds of programs can help people with dyslexia. Most of these programs use a method called *phonics* (FAH-niks). Phonics teaches the sounds of letters and how they look and sound when

A speech therapist is helping this girl to form speech sounds correctly. Her mother listens carefully and will help her practice at home.

they are put together to form words. Today, many schools in the United States do not teach phonics. They use the whole-word method, also called the "see and say" method, instead. The whole-word method teaches students words by the whole-word sound. Some schools teach some phonics along with the whole-word method. For dyslexics, phonics is the key to learning to read.

Experts are now starting to realize that phonics is important for all young readers, not just for those with reading problems. In fact, many companies have now created phonics games that have helped many kids learn to read.

Dyslexics seem to learn better when they use their senses of seeing, hearing, and touching. Saying words

Words as Pictures

Some specialists believe that dyslexia develops in children who naturally think in pictures rather than in words. Thinking in pictures is actually much faster, and it can produce very creative ideas. But it can be confusing when a child is learning words that do not suggest a picture, such as "a" or "and."

APPLE

AND

Tracing a sandpaper letter can help a child to feel what a "t" looks like.

out loud lets students hear how the words sound and feel the positions and movements of the mouth and tongue while saying them. Printing or writing words helps the students see how the letters and words look and also notice how the hand and fingers feel in writing each part of the words. This kind of **multisensory** approach helps dyslexics understand and remember information.

The first lesson may start with a basic understanding of the alphabet. The student looks at a picture of the letter "A," says its name aloud, and makes the sound it stands for. Then the child writes the letter in the air.

When students are learning how to form words, the teacher may use pictures of objects along with plastic letters to show the relationships between sounds and letters, and how they combine to form words. For example, a teacher may show a picture of a cat. The student practices spelling the word using plastic letters, as each letter is sounded out. He or she then says the whole word aloud and writes the word "cat" on a piece of paper or on the chalkboard.

Activity 2: Word Tricks

Dyslexics can learn little tricks to help them remember the difference between letters that look similar, such as "p" and "b." For example, they might think of these letters as "brother sounds" because their sounds are somewhat similar. Just as any two brothers are different, so are these letters. The letter "p" is the quiet brother, and "b" is the noisy brother.

Make each sound with your mouth. Can you tell the difference? Listen to the difference between the two sounds. Feel the difference on your lips and mouth. Learning tricks like these can help dyslexics improve their reading skills. A cute little story about certain letters can help a dyslexic remember how to sound them out.

Can you think of some interesting "stories" that could make it easier to tell the difference between other similar letters, such as "b" and "d" or "p" and "q"?

It is very important to teach dyslexics in a well-organized, step-by-step manner. They should start with simple ideas about language and gradually build up to more difficult information. For example, once students learn the sounds of letters, they can combine these letters and sounds to form words. They should also be able to break up words into syllables. Eventually, they will be able to put words together to make phrases and sentences.

Dyslexics can learn the same material as other students. They just need to learn it in a different way—and at their own speed. Dyslexics may have to work harder to succeed, but they can overcome their disability. Soon they can feel good about themselves and all that they have accomplished.

High-tech tools can help dyslexic children to learn more effectively.

What You Can Do

If you have dyslexia, you should know by now that you are a smart kid who happens to have a learning problem. That learning problem *can* be corrected. Hopefully, you are getting help for your condition, and you're on the road to success. Learning to read is only part of the problem though. Many dyslexics also have trouble

With the right help and lots of support, a child with dyslexia can do well in school.

staying organized and remembering things. Follow the suggestions listed below. They will help you listen better, remember things better, and get things done.

- Write notes to yourself. Colored Post-It® notes are great because you can stick them anywhere.
- Keep a notebook with a list of homework assignments and their due dates.
- If your parents ask you to do something, such as household chores, tell them to write you a note so that you won't forget.
- Use a calendar to keep track of the places you have to go.

Get organized! Make notes on a calendar to remind yourself of important events.

- Bring a tape recorder to class and record the lesson to make sure you don't miss any important information. (Check with the teacher first to make sure it's okay.)

Picking out your clothes the night before can save you time in the morning.

- Try to do tasks right away. If you put them off until later, you might forget about them.
- If you have to go somewhere at a certain time, set the kitchen timer. For instance, if you have to go to soccer practice in half an hour, set the timer for 30 minutes.
- When you finish your homework, always put your schoolbooks in the same special place. Then you won't have to hunt for them in the morning.
- Before you go to bed, decide what clothes you will wear the next day. That way you won't have to rush around in the morning.
- Develop a morning routine: go to the bathroom, brush your teeth, take a shower, get dressed, eat breakfast, get your books, and go to school.

Some dyslexics may prefer speaking into a tape recorder to remind themselves of important dates, chores, or assignments instead of writing them down in notes. However, as students improve their language and writing skills and feel more comfortable with writing, they may prefer making notes.

If children with dyslexia get the right kind of teaching and work hard, they can learn to read.

Practice! Overcoming reading problems is hard work, but it's well worth the effort.

Glossary

angular gyrus—an area in the brain that turns the visual image of words into sound patterns

attention deficit disorder (ADD)—a condition characterized by an inability to concentrate, pay attention, or control actions

Broca's area—an area in the front of the brain that directs the muscle movement so that you can speak the words once they are translated by Wernicke's area

cerebral cortex—the outermost layer of the brain. You use it to think, remember, make decisions, form sentences, and control body movements.

dyslexia—a learning disorder that makes it difficult to read, write, spell, speak, or listen

gene—a structure inside the body that passes on traits from parent to child

inherit—to pass on information by genes from parents to children

learning disability—a condition that makes it difficult to learn

MRI scan—a picture of the brain created by an imaging technique called magnetic resonance imaging.

multisensory—using more than one sense (seeing, hearing, tasting, smelling, or touching) at the same time

PET scan—a picture of the brain created by an imaging technique called positron emission tomography. The technique makes it possible to observe brain activity.

phoneme—a sound related to spoken language, such as a vowel or a consonant

phonics—a method that teaches the sounds of letters and how they look and sound when they are put together to form words

self-esteem—a feeling of satisfaction or pride a person has about himself or herself

syllable—part of a word that contains a vowel (a, e, i, o, u, or y)

Wernicke's area—an area in the back of the brain that helps us understand the meanings of words and string words together to speak in sentences

Learning More

Books

Davis, Ronald D. *The Gift of Dyslexia*. New York: Berkeley, 1997.

Gordon, Melanie Apel. *Let's Talk About Dyslexia*. New York: Rosen, Inc., 1999.

Hurford, Daphne M. *To Read or Not to Read*. New York: Simon & Schuster, 1998.

Moragne, Wendy. *Dyslexia*. Brookfield, Connecticut: Millbrook, 1997.

Nosek, Kathleen. *The Dyslexic Scholar: Helping Your Child Succeed in the School System*. Dallas, TX: Taylor Publishing, 1995.

Temple, Robin. *Your Child: Dyslexia*. Boston: Element Books, 1999.

Organizations and Online Sites

Dyslexia
http://specialed.about.com/education/specialed/msub37.htm
This online site includes many links concerning different aspects of dyslexia.

Dyslexia Online Magazine

http://members.aol.com/dddyslexia/magazine.html

An Internet magazine with articles for parents of dyslexics and adult dyslexics.

Dyslexia: Strategies to Overcome

http:/www.geocities.com/Athens/Atrium/5454/index.html

This site provides helpful tips on ways to improve reading, handwriting, spelling, and study skills.

Dyslexics.Net

http://www.dyslexics.net

This site has lots of links to information about dyslexia, chat rooms, message boards, organizations, and programs for helping dyslexics.

International Dyslexia Society

The Chester Building, Suite 382

8600 LaSalle Road

Baltimore, MD 21286-2044

http://www.interdys.org

This organization provides information about dyslexia. Its Web site has a kid's area with lots of information and fun activities.

Kids With Dyslexia

http://kidshealth.org/parent/medical/learning/dyslexia.html

This online site provides easy-to-read information about dyslexia.

Learning Disabilities Association of America
4156 Library Road
Pittsburgh, PA 15234-1349

National Center for Learning Disabilities, Inc.
381 Park Avenue South, Suite 1420
New York, NY 10016

Sam's Story of Life With Dyslexia
http://kidshealth.org/kid/health_problems/dyslexia.html
The story of 8-year-old Sam helps readers understand what dyslexia is and how it is treated.

SofDesign Dyslexia Services
http://www.sofdesign.com/dyslexia
This site provides links to video training programs, computer-based programs, books, and tapes for helping people with dyslexia.

The Dyslexia Index
http://pages.hotbot.com/edu/dyslexia.html
This site of The Dyslexia Society has articles, bulletin boards, and links to dyslexia information sites and organizations.

Index

Page numbers in *italics* indicate illustrations.

About the Authors

Dr. Alvin Silverstein is a professor of biology at the College of Staten Island of the City University of New York. **Virginia B. Silverstein** is a translator of Russian scientific literature. The Silversteins first worked together on a research project at the University of Pennsylvania. Since then, they have produced 6 children and more than 160 published books for young people.

Laura Silverstein Nunn, a graduate of Kean College, has been helping with her parents' books since her high-school days. She is the coauthor of more than thirty books on diseases and health, science concepts, endangered species, and pets. Laura lives with her husband Matt and their young son Cory in a rural New Jersey town not far from her childhood home.